Text
Bill Harris

Captions
Roger W. Hicks

Design
Teddy Hartshorn

Photography
Colour Library Books Ltd.
FPG International

Picture Researcher
Leora Kahn

Commissioning Editor
Andrew Preston

Editorial
David Gibbon

Director of Production
Gerald Hughes

CLB 2871
© 1992 Colour Library Books Ltd, Godalming, Surrey, England.
All rights reserved.
This 1992 editon published by Crescent Books,
distributed by Outlet Books, Inc., a Random House Company,
40 Engelhard Avenue, Avenel, New Jersey 07001.
Color separations by Scantrans (PTE) Ltd., Singapore
Printed and bound in Singapore
ISBN 0 517 07258 0
8 7 6 5 4 3 2 1

TENNESSEE

A PICTURE MEMORY

CRESCENT BOOKS
NEW YORK • AVENEL, NEW JERSEY

Imagine what would happen if all the people who helped make Tennessee what it is today were gathered together for a reunion in the ballroom of the Peabody Hotel in Memphis.

Andrew Jackson is in the center of the room, of course, probably comparing his uniform to the outfit Elvis Presley is wearing. Not far away is Andrew Johnson, the former tailor who became president, who is probably fascinated by Elvis's threads, too. Over there in the corner is Davy Crockett, comparing his long rifle to the carbine Sergeant Alvin York used to win the Medal of Honor in World War I. And here are Hank Williams and Roy Acuff chatting with the Cherokee Chief, Sequoia, who devised a written alphabet for his people, and Adolph Ochs, who went up north to build The New York Times from a penny sheet to America's Newspaper of Record. W.C. Handy is there with his trumpet, and so are the Fisk Jubilee Singers, who taught Queen Victoria to love American music. Meanwhile, Sam Houston is discussing the difference between Texas and Tennessee music with Uncle Jimmy Thompson, the fiddler who started the Grand Ole Opry, while former President James K. Polk reminisces about what fiddlin' was like in his day. John T. Scopes, the teacher who stood trial for teaching evolution to school children, is deep in conversation with Cordell Hull, who won the Nobel Peace Prize as Secretary of State during World War II. And Casey Jones, the high-rolling railroader, is comparing notes with Admiral David Farragut, whose order to go "full speed ahead" won the Battle of Mobile Bay for the Yankees in the Civil War. Sure, the Admiral fought on the wrong side, but so did thousands of other sons of Tennessee, so he can be forgiven. So can Jesse James. He didn't turn wrong until after he had turned his back on Tennessee, after all.

It would be quite a party. And when the time came to drink a toast to the Volunteer State, the Tennesseean most mentioned would be Jasper Newton Daniel.

Actually, he never liked being called Jasper and, when he was seven, he let it be known that henceforth he would only answer to the name of Jack. That was the year after he left home and went out into the world to seek his fortune, and found opportunity in the person of Dan Call, who ran a country store and operated a whiskey still on the side. Young Jack was fascinated by the still, but Dan figured he was much too young for the liquor business and kept the lad busy behind the counter of the store. Then one day, he suddenly changed his mind.

It happened when they were walking through the woods and their path was crossed by a rattlesnake. As the snake coiled to strike the store owner, the boy calmly picked up a stick and killed it with a crushing blow. Dan Call was not only grateful for having his life saved, but considered it a sign that this seven-year-old was as much a man as any of the ones who bought his whiskey. And with that, he not only gave Jack permission to watch the still, but volunteered to teach him everything he knew. It happened that nobody knew as much about making whiskey as Dan Call, but young Jack had no sooner mastered his secrets than Mr. Call had another change of heart. It was brought about by a beautiful young woman who called herself Lady Love.

The lady was a preacher. One of the best. Like hundreds of her kind, she traveled from town to town in 19th-century Tennessee bringing religion in her train. All of them preached against the evils of Demon Rum, but Lady

Love went beyond castigating men who drank the stuff. Even more evil in her eyes were the men who made it, and Dan Call knew that she was talking directly to him. With tears streaming down his cheeks he rushed to her side with a vow never to sell another drop as long as he lived.

He kept his promise. But Dan Call was no fool. Rather than destroying his distilling equipment, he offered to sell it, for a share of future profits, to Jack Daniel, now a teenager and the second-best whiskey-maker in all of Tennessee. But there was a problem. Dan had promised Lady Love and God that he'd stop selling whiskey, and he couldn't renege on the promise by allowing Jack to use his general store as an outlet. It meant that Jack had to look for a new market, and he found it across the border in Huntsville, Alabama.

Huntsville in 1860 wasn't what anyone would call a wide-open town, but they weren't opposed to taking a drink every now and then as long as it wasn't brought into town when anybody was looking. The fact was that liquor traffic was illegal, but as long as the police weren't on duty, there was no problem. The peace officers went home at midnight and didn't go back to work until sunup, which left plenty of time to stock the shelves at the local stores and taverns. Most nights found Jack Daniel making the rounds with his horse and wagon, and before long he and his silent partner were the toast of two states.

Jack was pretty well-known by then, even if only the insomniacs among his customers had ever seen him, and when the Government agents began moving in his direction, he made a business decision to play the game their way. The result was that the Jack Daniel Distillery became the first registered operation of its kind in the United States, and in a short time it was the second-largest sour mash distillery in Tennessee, if not the only legal one. By then he was turning thirty-three bushels of corn into eighty-three gallons of whiskey every day of the week. Every day but Sunday, of course. Religious principles had gotten him into this business and Jack Daniel wasn't the kind of man to tempt fate by working on the Sabbath.

In return, God was kind to Jack Daniel. His whiskey just kept getting better and better. He knew that corn was only one ingredient, and that the right water was just as important. It had to be clean and clear, with very little iron, and consistently cool, but not too cold. He found the perfect source in the little town of Lynchburg, which also had the advantage of good roads, and Huntsville wasn't too far south.

But he made his mark by going northwest in 1904, where they were having a World's Fair to celebrate the anniversary of the Louisiana Purchase, and entering his sour mash in a competition that included what most connoisseurs considered the world's best whiskeys. Most of the twenty-four entries were imported from Europe, and so were the judges, but when the tasting and sniffing was over, Jack Daniel won the gold medal for what they all agreed was the finest whiskey in the world.

When Jack died in 1911, long after he had turned the business over to his nephews, it looked as though the end had come for the world's finest whiskey, too. It wasn't that his successors didn't live up to his standards, but that the State of Tennessee had voted to prohibit the sale of alcohol. The boys moved the operation to St. Louis, but when the whole country went dry they were out of business.

The drought known as Prohibition ended in 1933, but by then the Lynchburg distillery had burned to the ground and the St. Louis operation had been sold. But Jack's nephew, Lem Motlow, was determined to carry on the family tradition. After rebuilding in Lynchburg, he set his first mash in 1938, and a year later the name of Jack Daniel was once again abroad in the land.

Even teetotalers can't resist the charm of the limestone spring cave and the rustic setting of the distillery and its nearby neighbor, George A. Dickel, which turns out some good "sippin' whiskey," too. But be careful. The locals feel it's their duty to welcome guests with a "Tennessee inch" of sour mash, which turns out to be about six ounces, and that's just for starters.

For rustic charm and quiet communing with nature, though, the best place in Tennessee, and arguably anywhere in the United States, is Great Smoky Mountains National Park. Even though it is the most-visited of all the National Parks, attracting more than ten million people a year, it is still a remarkable wilderness experience. Its eight hundred square miles absorb even holiday crowds with easy aplomb, and its eight hundred miles of hiking trails, including a seventy-mile stretch of the Appalachian Trail, make it possible to wander for hours with no intrusions except for an occasional wild turkey or a red fox. The Park is a wildlife sanctuary, with more than fifty species of mammals and two hundred different kinds of birds sharing the space with forty species of reptiles and seventy kinds of fishes.

The Park's most popular residents are the more than five hundred black bears who take special pleasure in preventing a population explosion among all those fish, and never seem more contented than when they stumble on a huckleberry patch. There are plenty of wild berries to keep them fat and happy, but not all the growing things in the Smokies are food for bears. The forests are filled with some 1,300 varieties of trees and shrubs, more than exist in all of Europe, including such tall trees as spruce and hemlock, poplars, maples and beautiful flowering magnolias. And under their branches the flower show in the spring includes thousands of dogwoods, rhododendrons, azaleas and laurel. But the show doesn't stop there. The climate is moist and warm, perfect for wildflowers, and hundreds of varieties compete for attention all summer long, leading up to fall when the leaves turn into brilliant colors that impresses even New Englanders who think they hold the patent on such displays.

Before the Park was established, most of the land was in the hands of timber companies, but it included more than 6,000 small farms, whose abandoned homesteads are still standing as a monument to Tennessee's past. The log cabins and mills were built by immigrants from England and Scotland, but the people who were already there when they arrived are part of the experience, too. Many of the visitors to the Great Smokies never leave their cars, preferring instead to follow tours described on tapes stuck into their cassette players. Significantly, one of the recorded tours is available in the language of the Cherokee. And why not? This was once their land, and some of their descendants live at the edge of the Park in North Carolina, on the Qualla Reservation, the biggest east of the Mississippi.

The Europeans who moved into their territory created an unusual culture all their own. In their isolated mountain homes they were closely knit, bound together by strong family ties and even stronger religious beliefs. It was a life of hard work, where loneliness was eliminated by frequent church meetings, barn raisings, quilting bees and corn huskings. And whenever they gathered together they brought along their harmonicas and their fiddles, and they sang hymns they remembered from the Old Country and ballads they made up as they went along.

What they started back in the hills has become a national institution that has made the name of one of Tennessee's great cities into an adjective that means "country music." Nashville has more banks than any city in the South, it has sixteen colleges and universities, five of the biggest religious publishers in the country and the biggest auto glass factory in the world. But although its boosters like to call it the "Athens of the South," there is hardly anyone in the country who doesn't think of Nashville as a sound they can't hear often enough.

The man who started it all was a seventy-year-old country fiddler who called himself Uncle Jimmy Thompson. One night in 1925 he wandered into the studios of Nashville's radio station WSM and asked if they'd like to put him on the air. Of course they would, and announcer George Dewey Hay, who later became better known as the "Solemn Old Judge," put Uncle Jimmy in front of a microphone and walked away. An hour later Uncle Jimmy was still going strong, and George asked him if he wasn't starting to get tired. "Heck no," said the old man. "I'm just gettin' started. I played all night last night at the State Fair."

The station's telephone lit up that night. Everybody loved Uncle Jimmy and they wanted more. A week later he had his own show, and with the help of such groups as the Gully Jumpers, the Fruit Jar Drinkers and the Possum Hunters, it quickly became the most popular radio program in Nashville. And not only in Nashville. WSM is a powerful, clear channel station whose signal travels all over the Eastern United States after the sun goes down, and country people who had migrated to cities like Chicago and Detroit found Jimmy Thompson and his friends the perfect cure for homesickness.

When they went home, they began making it a point to go by way of Nashville, where they could see the program "in person" as part of the studio audience. The station was forced to lease a movie theater to handle the crowds, and when they outgrew it they took over a former church and eventually built a 3,700-seat auditorium. But even that wasn't enough, and it wasn't possible to get a seat on less than a month's notice. And still the program didn't have an official name.

The four-hour program became a staple on the NBC Radio Network, and one Saturday night it went on the air behind a program of opera music, which gave announcer George Hay a perfect lead-in. "You've just been up in the air with grand opera," he said. "Now get down to earth with us for a performance of Grand Ole Opry!"

That night, a beautiful city of Southern Colonial Mansions, fine Victorian homes and some of the most beautiful gardens in the United States, became known as "Opryland." Completely forgotten was the fact it is the capital of Tennessee, the site of Andrew Jackson's beloved Hermitage and the place where another American president, Theodore Roosevelt, paid the ultimate compliment to the coffee at the Maxwell House Hotel by declaring it "good to the last drop." From then on Americans associated Nashville with Eddie Arnold and Ernest Tubb, Minnie Pearl and Red Foley. The words they remembered were the lyrics to such songs as "Rabbit in the Pea Patch," "Late Last Night My Willie Came Home," and "Chittlin' Cookin' Time in Cheatham County."

It wasn't very long before the big-time bands and singers were rushing into recording studios with their own version of what they smilingly called "hillbilly music," but down home in Nashville a couple of WSM engineers built their own recording studio and Opry stars had a new outlet for their talents. By the early 1940s, their records were selling as many as fifty thousand copies, which doesn't seem like much compared to today's million copy benchmark. But in those days, ten thousand was considered quite respectable and, in the years since, Nashville has become the second most important recording center in the country, and first in the production of country music.

One of the biggest of the early stars was Roy Acuff, a boy from the Smoky Mountains who never had a music lesson in his life, but saw his 1940s record of Wabash Cannonball gross $5 million at seventy-nine cents a copy. Nobody was more surprised than Roy. He always thought he'd grow up to be a professional baseball player. He was good enough to land a contract with the New York Yankees, but before he put on a uniform he collapsed from sunstroke and was forced to go back home.

While he was recovering, he taught himself to play the guitar and amused himself by writing and singing his own songs. Roy thought he was pretty good, but it took him three years to convince anyone else of it. When he did, it was a producer of the Opry, and after one appearance Roy Acuff became a regular on the program. Like the others who appeared with him, his songs were mostly about broken hearts and lost loves, and that was just the ticket for GIs far away from home in World War II Europe.

They made him the most popular singer of the era, regularly edging out even Frank Sinatra and Bing Crosby, both in terms of record sales and popularity polls. More than the Grand Ole Opry itself, Roy Acuff made the Nashville Sound a national passion and set a standard for all the stars the city has produced in the half century since.

Acuff was also largely responsible for relegating the word "hillbilly" to history. It quietly vanished in the 1950s, to be replaced by the more respectable-sounding "country-western" designation. And before long it gave birth to something new and different. And though the new sound came from several different sources, the one that counted most came from Memphis, Tennessee.

An engineer named Sam Phillips built a studio in Memphis to record local blues singers for the small but growing demand by record companies for that special Southern sound. But not everyone who used his facilities had a recording contract in mind, and when a kid named Elvis Presley said he wanted to record a song as a birthday present for his mother, Sam was happy to oblige. He was even happier when he heard the kid's voice, and he suggested that they work together with an instrumental backup. It took them a year and a half to come up with the right formula, but they finally hit it with a song called "That's All Right," written by another Memphian, Big Boy Crudup. It was a huge success in Memphis, as were the other songs Elvis recorded for Phillips's Sun Records. It was only a matter of time before the boy moved on to bigger things. But, as if to prove the old adage that you can take the boy out of the country, but you can't take the country out of the boy, although he was called the King of Rock and Roll, nothing ever pleased Elvis Presley more than to be called a Tennessean.

Burgess Falls (facing page), near Murfreesboro, are a beautiful reminder of one of Tennessee's most abundant and attractive resources: the pure, clear water of the state. Waterfalls, from trickles gurgling at the side of the road, to great falls which roar throughout the year, are among the most attractive features of the state, as are the rivers and rills that feed them.

Tennessee is rich in history. Fort Watauga (top left) is a restored pioneer fort; Rocky Mount (below and bottom left) was one of the finest houses in the area when it was built in 1770; Allandale at Kingsport (facing page top), was first built in 1847 but has been almost completely rebuilt since; and the covered bridge at Elizabethton (facing page bottom) is over a century old. Bristol (left) grew from the Colonial trading post at Sapling Grove, and Jonesboro (above and overleaf) is the oldest town in Tennessee.

Rugby (above, left and facing page), was founded as a community for the younger sons of the English aristocracy and gentry and named after the famous English school. The Abraham Lincoln Museum at Harrogate (top left) has wax-figure tableaux of scenes from Lincoln's life, while the Andrew Johnson National Historic Site (bottom left) at Greeneville has his original tailor's shop and a museum on one side of the road, and the house he bought in later life on the other. Below: Northrap Falls in Colditz Cove State Natural Area.

Facing page: Knoxville City County Building, seen from the East Tennessee Baptist Hospital (top), downtown Knoxville from the southern shore of Fort Loudon Lake (center), and James White Fort, dwarfed by skyscrapers (bottom). The Great House of the Fort, dating from 1786, is the only eighteenth-century building to have survived in Knoxville. Below: one of the outbuildings of the Fort, with its typical log walls and stone chimney. Fire, termites, and decay often mean that only the chimney survives intact from many Colonial and Pioneering period buildings.

17

The town of Pigeon Forge (below) is close to Gatlinburg, one of the most popular resort towns in the Tennessee mountains. The nearby Old Mill (overleaf) was already an established business in 1861, when the War Between the States began. Facing page: Gatlinburg can be seen from the top of Crockett Mountain (bottom), which is served by a chair-lift (top). There are almost eight times as many beds in Gatlinburg's many hotels and motels (center) as there are permanent residents in the city: 23,000 beds, as compared with 3,000 people!

The "smoke" of the Great Smoky Mountains (these pages) is the blue haze that surrounds the countless trees that cover the mountain slopes. The views are from the Newfound Gap Road (facing page top); Grotto Falls (facing page bottom); Rainbow Falls, near Cherokee Orchard (above); a peaceful stream near Greenbrier (below); Cades Cove (top right); the Roaring Fork Motor Nature Trail (right); and tobacco drying in stooks in the Wear Valley (bottom right). Overleaf: clouds add to the image of the Great Smokies.

27

BATTLE OF CHATTANOOGA, 2D DAY, NOV. 24.

The delicate beauty of Falls Creek Falls (facing page) contrasts with the sprawling majesty of the Burgess Falls near Murfreesboro (overleaf). Tennessee water is the secret of Jack Daniels whiskey, maturing in charred-oak casks in Lynchburg (right), and Tennessee water carved the Sewanee Natural Bridge (bottom right). Stone's River, Murfreesboro (top right), was the scene of a savage battle of the Civil War. The wildness of Buzzard's Roost (above) contrasts with the handsome buildings of Tennessee Technical University (below).

The phrase "Grand Ole Opry" was first used in 1925 on WSM radio station, though the roots of country music go back to the original settlers of Tennessee. Today, "Opryland" is central to Nashville, with its own Hall of Fame and Museum (facing page top); the Opryland Theater by the Lake (facing page bottom, and right); the Opryland Juke Box Theater (top right); and the Encore Theater (bottom right). There are shops all along Music Way, too, some bearing famous names.

The Hermitage (below), the tranquil, historic home of President Andrew Jackson, is also in Nashville. Though the house was first built in 1819, it had to be rebuilt after a fire in 1835. The mansion is only one of many handsome buildings in and around Nashville. Others include the State Capitol (overleaf); and (facing page) Belle Mead (top); Traveler's Rest (center); and Two Rivers (bottom). Built in 1853, Belle Mead was until 1902 the principal center of horse-breeding in Tennessee, which like Kentucky is renowned for horses.

Classical influences can be seen in the Doric colonnades of Nashville's War Memorial Building (top left and above) and in the elegantly-proportioned Capitol (below); but few other cities have a replica of the Athenian Parthenon like the one in Nashville's Centennial Park (left). The downtown area is, however, mostly modern (facing page top), while the architecture on Music Row (facing page bottom) is ordinary. Busy roads lead from the Victory Memorial Bridge (bottom left) and (overleaf) is a huge truck stop on the Interstate.

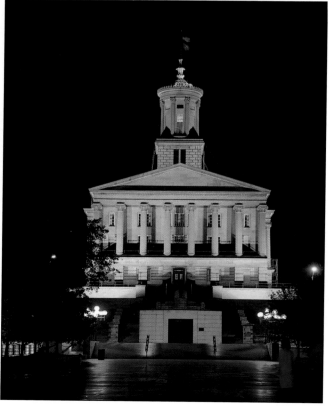

A cannon guards the river (facing page top) at Fort Donelson National Battlefield (above), near Dover. Facing page top: Clarksville. Davy Crockett's last home at Rutherford (below) is less imposing than the boyhood home of James K. Polk (above right). The Casey Jones Museum (bottom right) commemorates another folk hero. Waynesboro Natural Bridge (right) is one of several in Tennessee. Overleaf: the bridge at Paris Landing.

Riverboats may be safe and stately today, but in the latter half of the nineteenth century the stern-wheeler operators used to vie with one another to provide the fastest service, as well as the most luxurious and highly-decorated boats. Racing was in deadly earnest: boiler explosions were frequent as they were stoked way beyond their safe limits, and the steamboats were even more dangerous than their fast-emerging rivals, the railroads. These pages: Memphis Queen III, Memphis Queen and Samuel Clemens. Overleaf: Memphis Queen and the Memphis Showboat.

The Victorian district around Adams Avenue in Memphis contains many fine old houses (top left and bottom left). Graceland (left), home of Elvis Aaron Presley (above), however, attracts many more visitors. Today, Elvis' home is something of a shrine and many thousands of people come to see "The King's" memorial (below), the clothes he wore (facing page bottom), and the vehicles he drove (facing page top), and the interior of the house where he lived.

The unromantically-named Mud Island lies in the river beside Memphis. On the island are fountains and lakes (below), and a scale model of the Mississippi River itself (facing page center) including the Mississippi Delta (facing page bottom). The model is five city blocks long, and compresses the whole 900 miles of the river from Illinois to the sea into that distance. Access to the mainland is via a bridge with a suspended monorail train beneath it (facing page top). Overleaf: an aerial view of the dynamic downtown area of Memphis, with Mud Island in the foreground.

The delicacy of the fountain (left and facing page top) is hard to reconcile with the name "Mud Island." The Mid American Plaza (above, below and top left) is a select part of downtown Memphis, while the musical heritage of the city is clear from the street advertisements (bottom left and facing page bottom). Overleaf: city lights sparkle and reflect in the water, the half-seen riverboats contrasting with the ever-present cranes on the skyline, building the future. Following page: the sun gleams through the intricate steel network of the I-40 bridge.